2

WHAT'S THEIR KINGDOM?

By: Juliene McCormick

Illustrated by: Claire Thoele

I think this book is about us! We should help!

3

to my children and grandchildren

"Heaven is under our feet as well as over our heads."
Henry David Thoreau

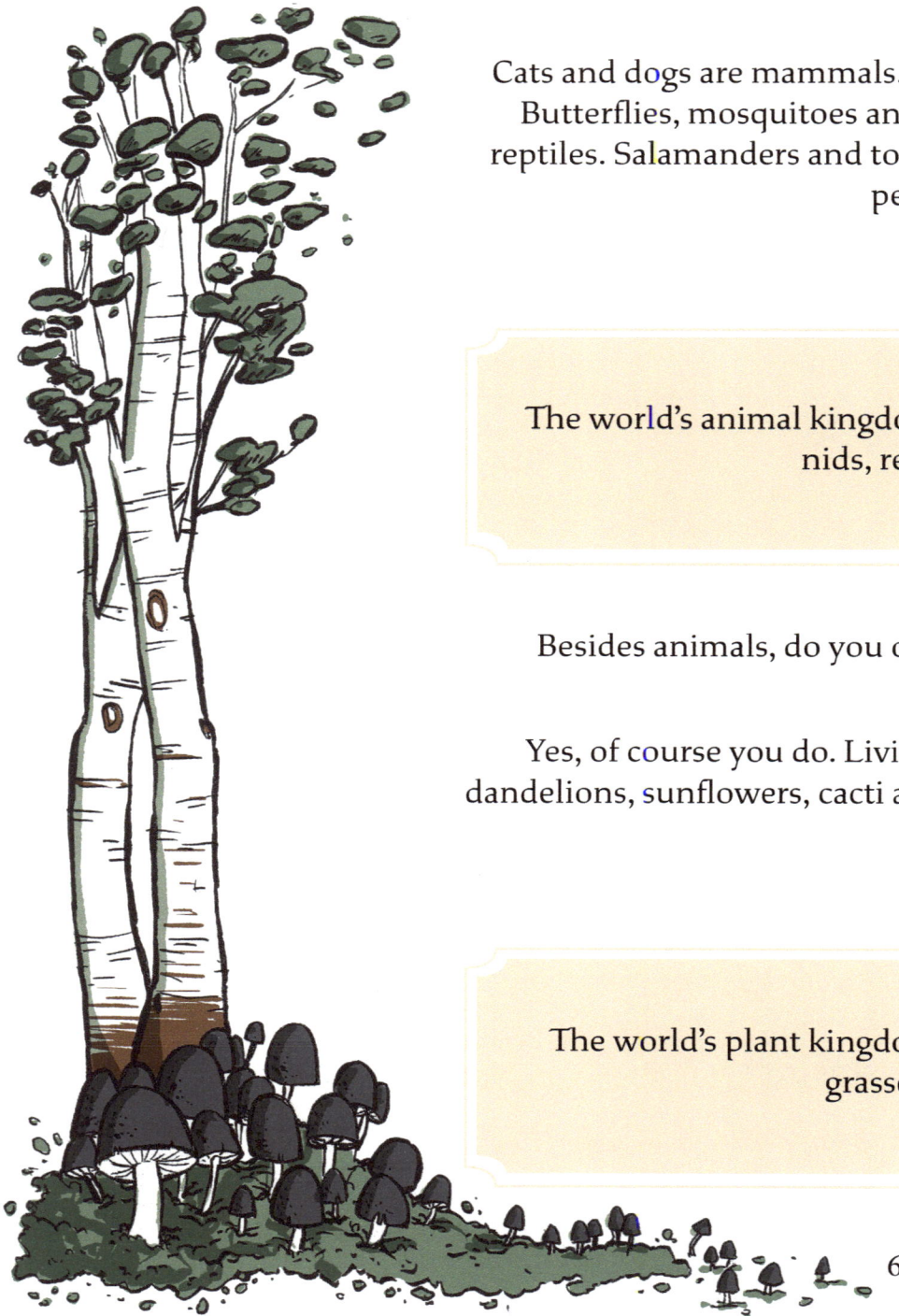

Cats and dogs are mammals. Carp and salmon are fish. Spiders and ticks...arachnids. Butterflies, mosquitoes and beetles are - do **you** know? Alligators and snakes are reptiles. Salamanders and toads... amphibians. Black-capped chickadees, parrots and pelicans are... **you** say it Reader!

It's a FACT!

The world's animal kingdom has all different kinds of mammals, insects, arachnids, reptiles, birds, fish and amphibians.

Besides animals, do you observe other things that grow and live in our world?

Yes, of course you do. Living things that grow from seeds, such as trees, grasses, dandelions, sunflowers, cacti and the tasty treats we eat daily, like any fruit or vegetable. They are all plants.

It's a FACT!

The world's plant kingdom is made of many different kinds of trees, bushes, grasses, flowers, vegetables and fruits.

So, do you think everything growing and living is either an animal or a plant?

I can almost hear you saying, "What about us kids?" "We're living and growing, and we are not animals or plants."

Actually, children *are* living, breathing and growing animals. That sounds funny, doesn't it?! You were born alive, and you have hair on your skin. For this and other reasons, boys and girls are mammals, right along with moms, dads, grandmas, grandpas, cousins, AND dogs, cats, bears, elephants, guinea pigs and many other hair-bearing creatures.

But, Mammal Readers, there is still something else besides *plant* and *animal*, very visible in our beautiful world. And it is a growing, living, changing thing.

Can you guess what it might be?

OK, I will tell you. It is...

MUSHROOMS

Yes, it's us!
We are not unchanging, like a rock or a stick.
We grow and can make more of ourselves.
Mushrooms are a living thing.

It's understandable that there is some confusion on exactly what 'group' we mushrooms belong to. After all, just like plants we don't move around. And besides that, many of us also enjoy living on damp forest floors.

Then, we are a bit animal-like too, because we must eat to stay alive. But scientists tell us that even though we have some similar traits, we are neither animal *nor* plant.

If you can't say,
"A mushroom's an animal,"
and you can't say:
"A mushroom's a plant,"
well then, what *are* they?

We make up a large portion of a group of very unique, living things.

Our kingdom is called...

THE FUNGI KINGDOM

Just as there are many kinds of animals and plants, there are a multitude of us mushrooms in the world -- over 10,000 to be exact!

Mammal Readers, have you ever heard these words: portabella, porcini, enoki? These are the names of just a few types of mushrooms, and I love how they sound.

Repeat after me, as fast as you can -- portabella, porcini, enoki; portabella, porcini, enoki.

Sounds like we're speaking a foreign language. doesn't it?!

PORTABELLA

PORCINI

ENOKI

9

Mushrooms can be found all around the world and can often be seen right in your own back yard. Have you ever spied us growing up the side of a tree or nestled on the ground within a clump of damp leaves?

Now wait a minute "Funguys." (May I call you that?) Before you go on, I want to tell the readers what I do when *I* spy mushrooms.

No matter where I happen to be--whether walking in my yard, at a park or in the woods--I always have an eye out for mushrooms. I photograph them to capture the next great picture for my collection.

Look at the amazing cluster of bracket fungi in the picture below: I spied them growing up the side of a tree in the state of Wisconsin.

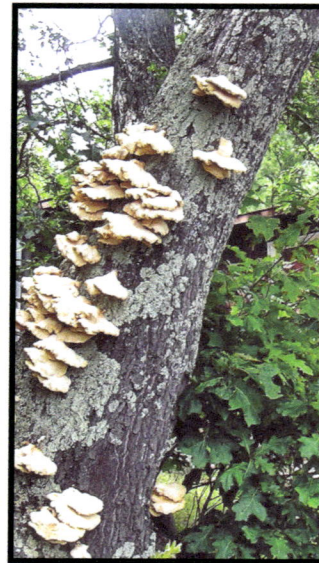

10

I found the white beauties you see in this photo, while taking a walk at the Mississippi Palisades State Park in Northern Illinois.

Never again have I seen any quite the same. I suppose that's part of the reason why the experience of finding mushrooms is so special...each one is different, like you!

The part of a mushroom that you can see, above the ground, is called the fruiting body of a fungus. (One fungi is called a fungus, just like one teeth is called a tooth and one cacti is called a cactus...you get the idea!) This fruiting part of a fungus is sort of like an apple being the fruit of an apple tree.

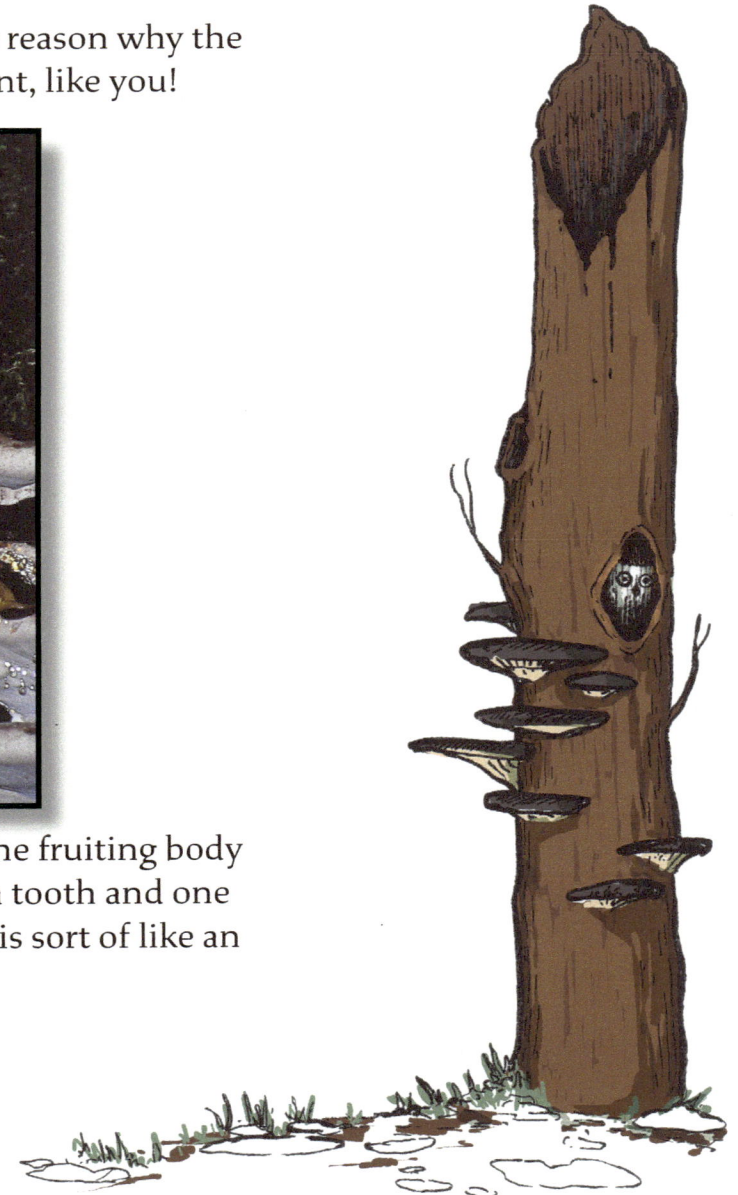

Just like there are different kinds of apples, the fruiting part of mushrooms comes in many different sizes, shapes and colors. They can be as small as an ant or as large as a cat.

The photo of the large mushroom you see above was taken in the state of Missouri. It showed up one day right in my friend Audrey's front yard. Doesn't it almost look like a large flower blossom?

13

While most of us are white, cream-colored and brown, very colorful mushrooms also exist in the world - red, orange, blue, violet, green or even black.

Like these little green ones I found growing out the end of a log in a woodpile!

Mammal Readers, many mushrooms start out looking like small buttons. Then some will grow into stalks with a cap on top.

As our caps become larger, they unfold like an umbrella, with small plates called gills fanning out underneath.

See the gills, stalks and caps in this photo?

GILL

CAP

STALK

Remember the large mushroom I found in the front yard of my friend Audrey's house? It looked like a flower blossom? That's an example of a fungi *without* gills. Their fruiting bodies have pores or tubes on the underside instead. This kind of fungi is called a *polypore*.

I mentioned that mushrooms can make more of themselves.
"Funguys," would you like to tell them how it happens?

Sure. Here's how it works: Our main purpose in life is to produce spores or "tiny seeds".

Itty, bitty, tiny spores, no larger than a speck of dust, are released out of our cap-- millions, just waiting for a breeze to blow 'em into the air! New mushrooms can develop then, as long as the spores fall on a warm, wet area, such as rotting wood or layers of wet leaves.

Mammal Readers, a lot is always happening *underground* in the development of more fungi.

A mushroom that pops up actually has "branches" growing underneath it. They are like fine white threads all tangled together.

This part is called the mycelium (my-SEAL-ee-um).

Just imagine an apple tree growing entirely underground, its trunk and branches buried. The only time you'd even know a tree is there would be when an apple pops up out of the ground.

That's not how apples grow, of course, but it's exactly how mushrooms do!

If the mushroom's mycelium underground gets enough nourishment, it may live for hundreds or even thousands of years growing to be very large.

(Are you seeing why scientists really did, at one time, think mushrooms **were** plants?)

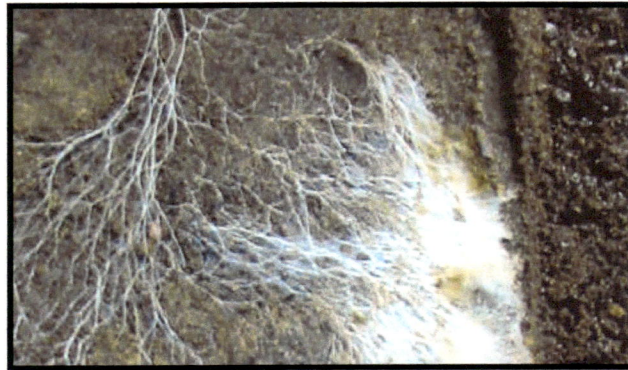

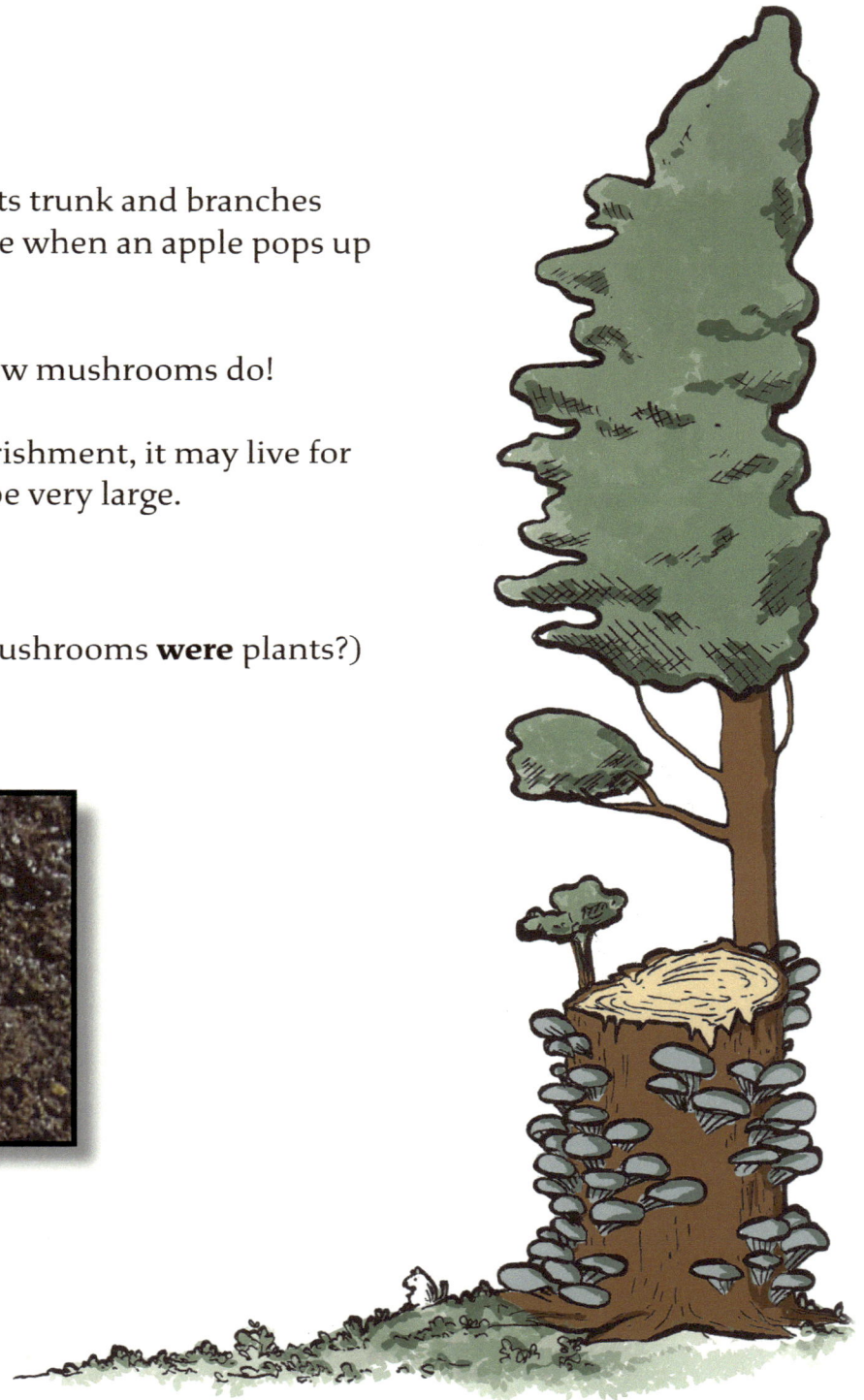

17

Mycologists (those who research and study fungi) know of one amazing underground mycelium that is as big as the entire state of Illinois! It was discovered back in 1998 in the Blue Mountains of Oregon. That mycelium was the size of 1,665 football fields! So...

It's a FACT!

Fungi have the potential to be the largest living things on earth.

I could have told them that!

Most people think of the blue whale as the largest living animal, and the giant sequoia as the largest living plant, but they're not nearly as large as this humongous, sprawling fungus found in Oregon.

18

So what would this monstrous fungus eat to stay alive?

"Funguys," what does any mushroom eat to stay alive?

Well, Mammals, here's where we fungi are really different from plants and animals. We can't make our own food or hunt for our food.

Brace yourself. Here's what we like: Fungi really have an appetite for dead plants and animals.

"Yuck," you say?

Mushrooms have to eat to grow and stay alive just like you kids do. But the problem is, with their stomachs being on the outside of their bodies, they have to rely on the underground mycelium for help to bring them their food.

20

The mycelium gets the nutrients to our fruiting mushroom parts from the rotting plants that are lying around it. That's how it works for us in the fungi kingdom.

Mammal Readers, this whole process can actually be very helpful to the earth's forest lands. After all, when fungi help decompose dead trees, more space is made for new little trees to grow.

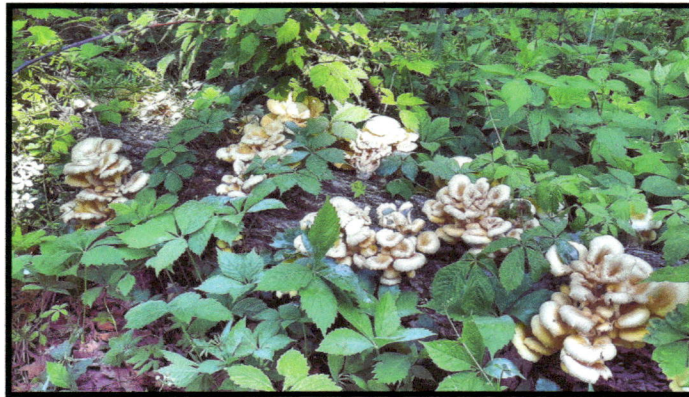

We help trees in other ways also. About 20 years ago, an ecologist named Suzanne Simard made a great discovery. Her research revealed that trees actually communicate with each other.

How do they accomplish *that*, you are wondering!? We are proud to declare -- it is via us fungi!!

Mycelium acts like an underground railway system in the tree communication process. It absorbs rich nutrients from the soil surrounding a healthy tree and spreads those nutrients to the soil near an unhealthy tree.

How amazing is that?! And then because trees help nourish fungi, it makes for a lovely *symbiotic* relationship: fungi helping trees survive and trees helping fungi survive.

HOWEVER...I must be honest and tell you that some fungi behave in a way that can be harmful. Have you ever heard about athlete's foot or ringworm?

Athlete's foot and ringworm are nasty fungi that can start to grow on YOU and eat your skin to stay alive.

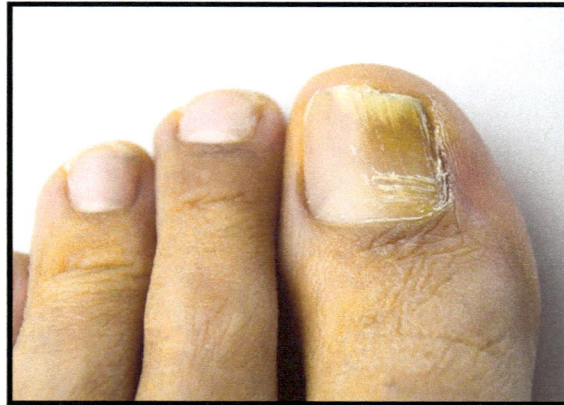

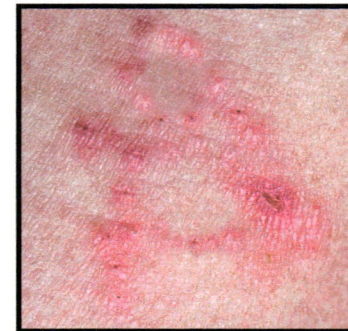

Thankfully, doctors have special medicines to help treat these problems.

And speaking of medicines, I am so pleased to share that medicines like penicillin and other antibiotics are made from...

FUNGI!

If you've ever had an ear infection or strep throat, you probably took antibiotics to get well -- thanks to the helpful fungi.

LETS SAY IT: THANKS FUNGI!

Another good thing about mushrooms is that they help provide animals with food to eat. Since you are a part of the animal kingdom, I must ask, "Do you eat mushrooms... like on your pizza or in your salads?"

Morels, shiitakes, oysters , buttons, portabellas and porcinis are all great to eat.

But we must be responsible and warn that some mushrooms are not!

The fly agarics, Mammal Children, are very attractive, beautiful really, but they are extremely poisonous, if eaten.
Please remember this!

So, Mammal Readers, some fungi taste great, but others could harm you.

Fly Agarics

NEVER eat any wild mushroom unless an adult tells you it's safe.

THAT'S A FUNGI RULE!

But it certainly is always okay and safe to observe us!

Encourage them, Author!

Mammal Readers, I do hope you will go outside sometime very soon and search for mushrooms.

Personally, I find that discovering one (or dozens of them) is always an unexpected and slightly mysterious surprise. I believe that you will find that to be true also.

I'll just say it:

IT'S AN ADVENTURE YOU'LL NOT WANT TO MISS!

When you do find them, snap a photo or sketch a picture of your fungi treasure (if you like drawing), and send it to me, for my collection.

Better yet, start your own collection of mushroom photos and drawings!

To go on a mushroom hunt, I recommend you pick a sunny day right after there have been a few rainy days. That's the best time to search for them.

Make sure to not only look, but also gently touch the growing living fungi things -- feel their sponginess and observe the underside closely.

See the gills, radiating from their stem like rays of light around the sun.

It was about 4:00 in the afternoon when I looked up and saw this spectacular mushroom high over my head -- growing right out of the branch of a tree.

Those gills and sturdy stem were amazing to see from down below!

27

When you find fungi, it won't do any harm to choose one, pick off its cap from the stem and take it home. Put the mushroom cap, gill side down, on a piece of construction paper. Place a bowl or jar over the cap and leave it covered overnight.

Then, see what you find the next morning, when you carefully lift the cap off the paper.

Our final word to you, speaking on behalf of all mysterious, amazing mushrooms is this -- when you do discover us, we want to hear you give a shout and cry -

I SPY YOU FUNGI!

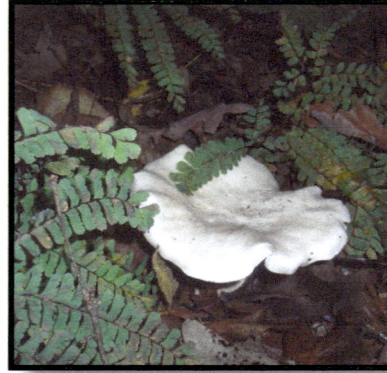

FUNGI SONG

Fungi, fungi,

You are a friend, I know

You help decompose old trees

So new little ones can grow

You really don't look so scary

Might be spongy

Never hairy

Often a cap

A stem

And gills,

Little fungi friend of mine

SOME PHOTOS FROM MY FUNGI JOURNAL

33

37

39

40

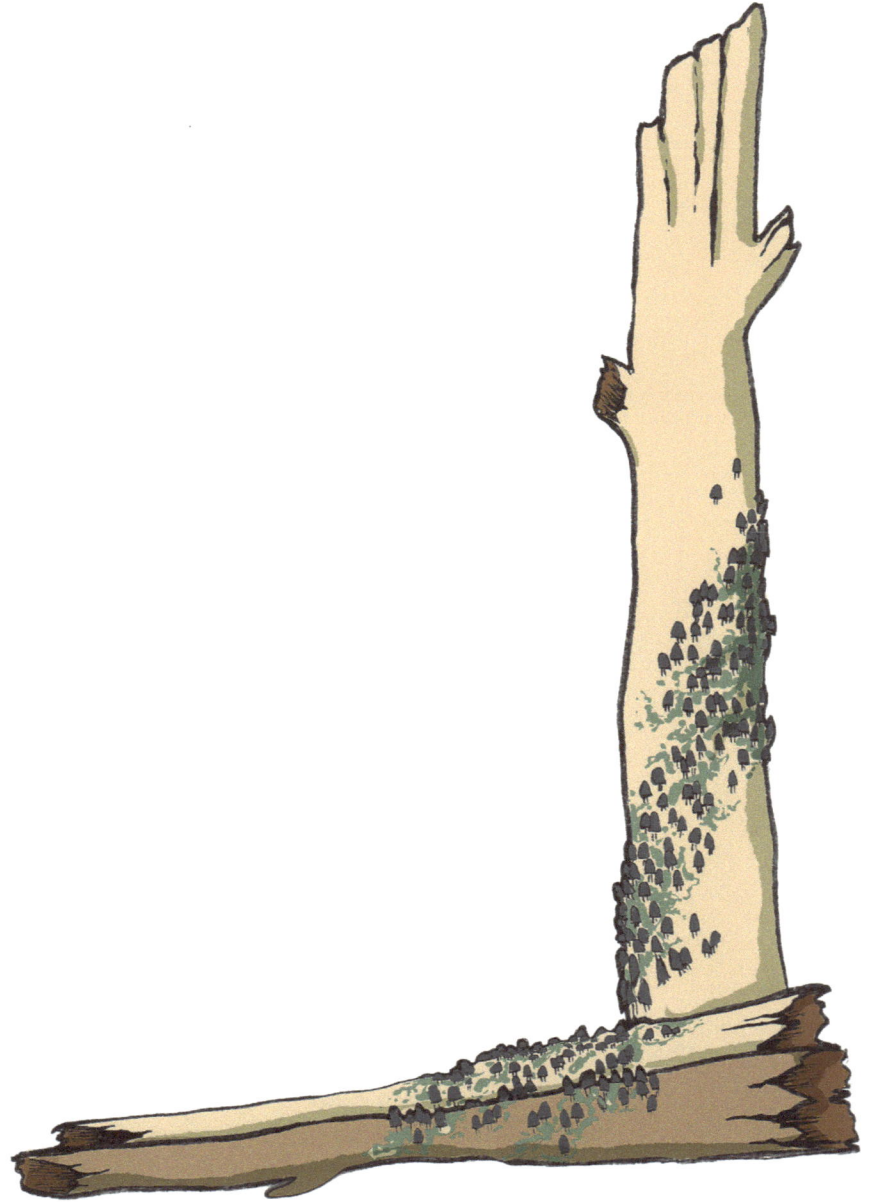

43

PORCINI
EDIBLE

FLY AGARIC
NON-EDIBLE

DEATH CAP
NON-EDIBLE

BLACK TRUMPET
EDIBLE

HONEY
EDIBLE

LOBSTER
EDIBLE

MOREL
EDIBLE

YELLOW FOOT
EDIBLE

KING STROPHARIS
EDIBLE

CONOCYBE FILARIS
NON-EDIBLE

DESTROYING ANGEL
NON-EDIBLE

HEN OF THE WOODS
EDIBLE

BLEWIT
EDIBLE

CHANTERELLE
EDIBLE

SHAGGY MANE
EDIBLE

Do the spores from various types of mushrooms look different?
Are the spore sizes different?
Does the color of a mushroom affect the color of the spores?
Make a prediction. Make a hypothesis. Draw a conclusion.
Include drawings in your journal.

Color this picture of kids on a mushroom hunt.

NOW YOU CAN DRAW A "FUNGUY"!

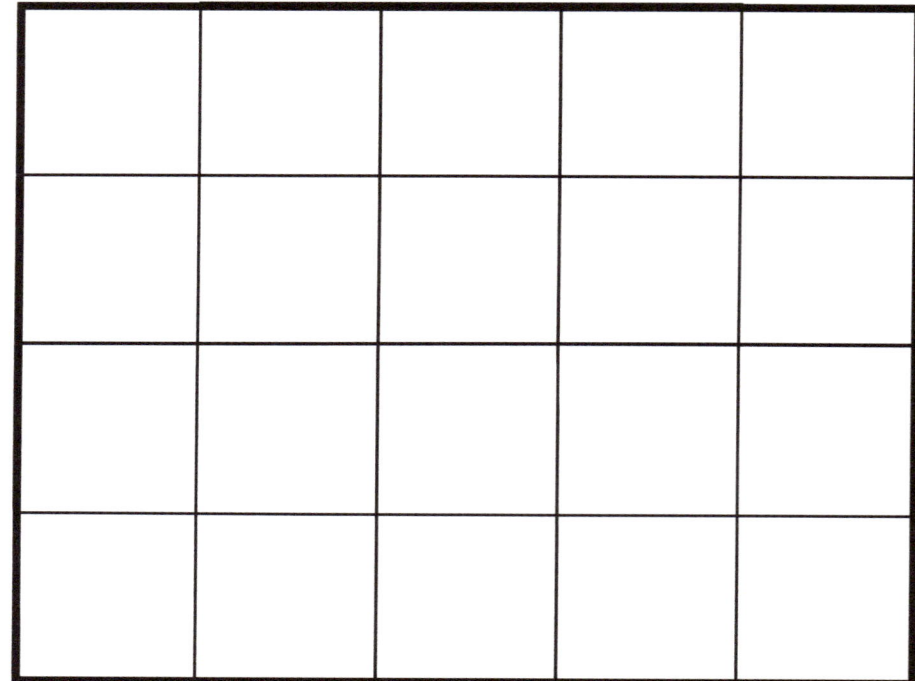

HOW TO DRAW A "FUNGUY"!

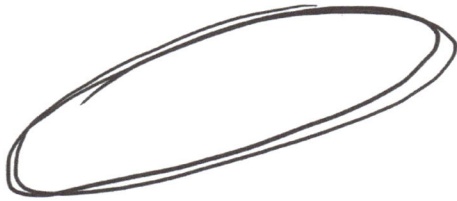

Step 1: Draw an oval

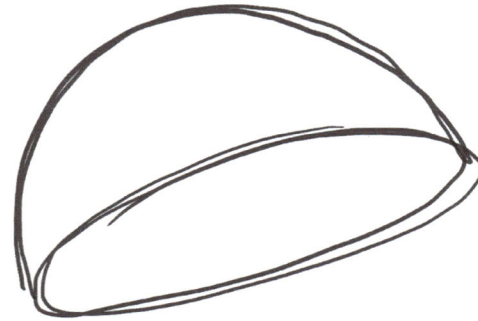

Step 2: Draw a half circle on top

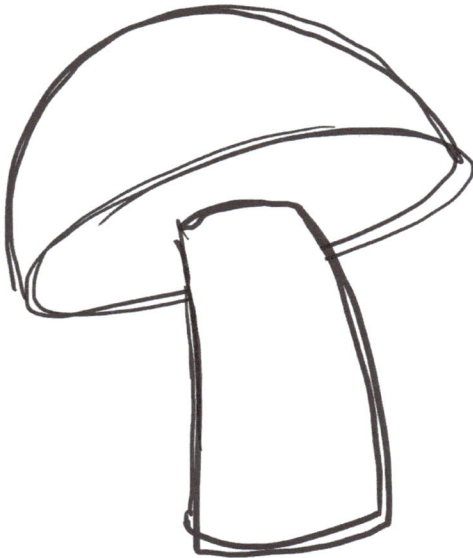

Step 3: Add a Stem

47

Step 4: Add details. Be creative!

About the Author:

As an educator, Juliene McCormick encouraged students to be curious about nature and embrace its exploration. She frequently integrated art and music into all curricular instruction.

Her appreciation of Mother Nature began during childhood, growing up on a 60 acre farm in the rolling hills of Missouri. There she ate and drank, fresh or preserved, only what the gardens, fruit trees and animals provided.

Juliene has called a quaint river-town in the NW corner of Illinois her home for many years. The beautiful Mississippi Palisades State Park, with limestone bluffs overlooking the sprawling river, is close by…a great playground for discovering nature's treasures. But no matter where Juliene is exploring, she always has her camera ready for capturing the next unique fungi photo.

About the Illustrator:

Claire Thoele grew up in Northern Illinois where she loved hunting for morels every spring and drawing the rest of the year. She currently lives in Iowa City with her husband and dog.

Claire still spends most of her time drawing, but enjoys taking long walks in the woods with her boys and finding fungi there.

www.ingramcontent.com/pod-product-compliance
Lightning Source LLC
Chambersburg PA
CBHW040711150426

42811CB00061B/1821